To our daughter Christian,

We pray you remember everything we teach, invest all that we deposit, and be empowered by whose you are.

-MAMA & DADDY

Every day that I'm not with you;
I pray that you are safe.
I hope that you remember,
to be passionate and brave.

Be kind, smart, and helpful;
creative, strong, and sweet
Also to be fearless and confident
when you speak.

But there are times when you must know
when, where, and how to be
So that your decisions are wise,
to make it home to me.

Unfortunately, everyone isn't kind, honest, or cares.
Regardless, the love of Christ is our job to share.

When on patrol, it's my job to make everyone feel safe, but sometimes on the news it doesn't always seem that way.

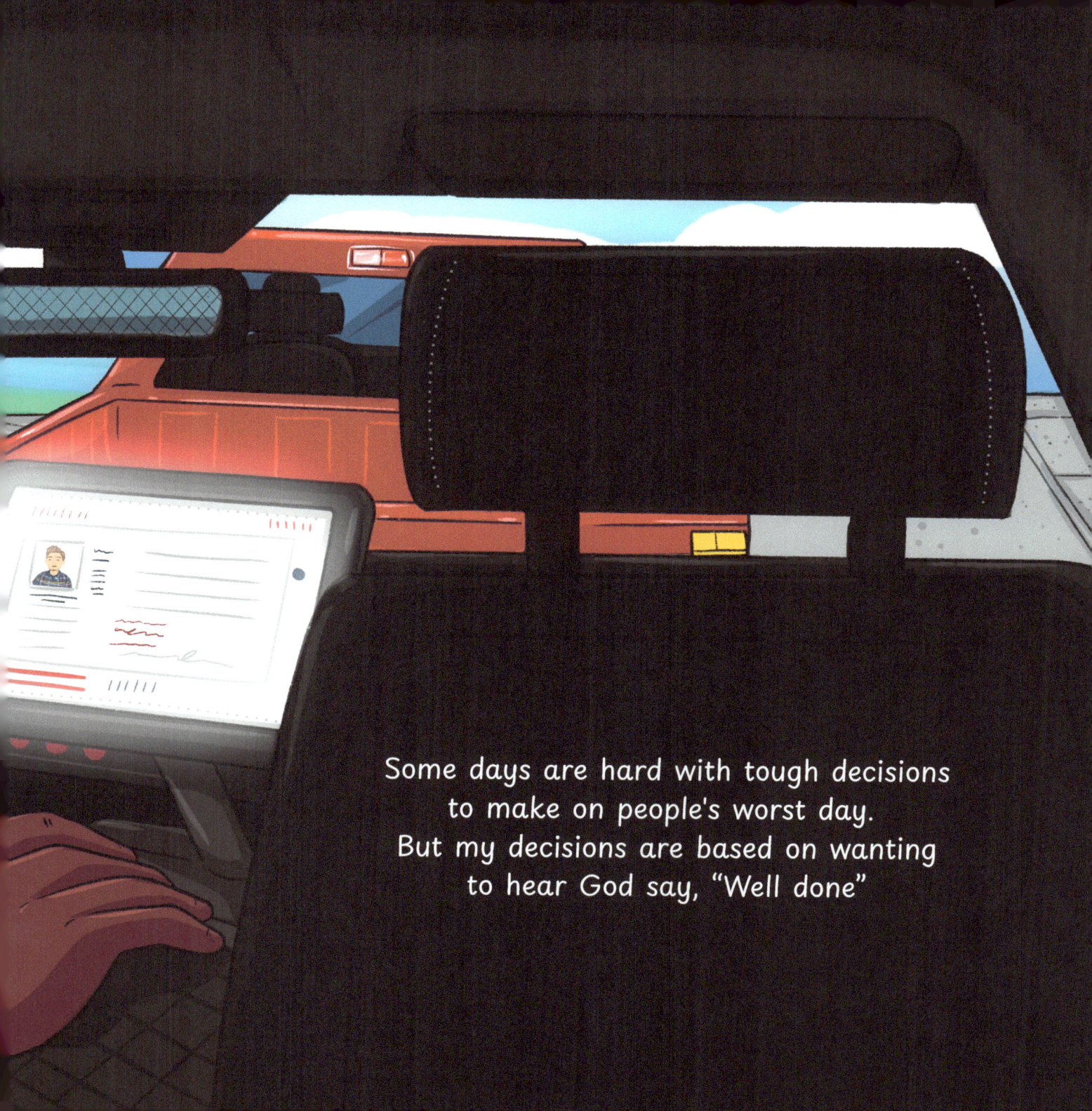

Some days are hard with tough decisions to make on people's worst day. But my decisions are based on wanting to hear God say, "Well done"

I'm HIS first, yours second, and a police officer third. Keeping my priorities intact with one single word... FAITH

in God that through the day,
he keeps us both safe from harm.
So that at the end of the day
your smile and hug are warm.

It took no time for you to be comfortable seeing a uniform blue, but it will take less time to be uncomfortable if complying isn't what you do.

🌐 https:littlechristianacademy.com

www.ingramcontent.com/pod-product-compliance
Lightning Source LLC
Chambersburg PA
CBHW051516110526
44582CB00007B/138